For Jennif

as you.

To remember . . . .

All our love forever!

Mom & Dad

B & J

August 15, 1999

The Bride's Book

BY
MARCIA O. LEVIN

GALAHAD BOOKS
NEW YORK

ILLUSTRATIONS

Marc Chagall
COUPLE ABOVE ST. PAUL
St. Paul de Vence, Artist's Collection
Photograph: Art Resource

Pablo Picasso
THE LOVERS
1923
51 $\frac{1}{4}$ X 38 $\frac{1}{4}$"
National Gallery of Art, Washington, D.C., Chester Dale
Collection, 1962
© S.P.A.D.E.M., Paris/V.A.G.A., New York 1985

Lucas van Leyden
The BETROTHAL
undated
oil on wood
11 $\frac{13}{16}$ X 12 $\frac{9}{16}$"
Koninklijk Museum voor Schone Kunsten, Antwerp

Attributed to The Washing Painter
HYDRIA; WOMAN AND EROS (BRIDE RECEIVING
PRESENTS)
5th century B.C.
terracotta
Attic, red-figured
h. 12 $\frac{1}{4}$"
The Metropolitan Museum of Art, New York. Rogers Fund,
1922

Bilasper or Mandi (India)
A MARRIAGE PROCESSION PASSING THROUGH A
BAZAAR
c. 1680
Private collection

Grandma Moses
A COUNTRY WEDDING
1951
oil on Masonite
17 X 22"
Copyright © 1973, Grandma Moses Properties Co., New
York

Henri Rousseau
THE WEDDING
c. 1905
oil on canvas
63 $\frac{3}{4}$ X 44 $\frac{1}{2}$"
The Louvre, Paris
Photograph: Service de documentation photographique de
la Réunion des musées nationaux, Paris

Charles Webster Hawthorne
THE TROUSSEAU
1910
oil on canvas mounted on wood
40 X 40"
The Metropolitan Museum of Art, New York

Norman Rockwell
MARRIAGE LICENSE, 1955
oil on canvas
45 $\frac{1}{2}$ X 42 $\frac{1}{2}$
Printed by permission of the Estate of Norman Rockwell
Copyright © 1955 Estate of Norman Rockwell
Photograph: Courtesy of The Norman Rockwell Museum at
The Old Corner House, Stockbridge, Massachusetts

Rembrandt van Rijn
THE JEWISH BRIDE
c. 1665–68
oil on canvas
47 $\frac{7}{8}$ X 65 $\frac{1}{2}$"
The Rijksmuseum, Amsterdam

William Hogarth
THE WEDDING OF STEPHEN BECKINGHAM AND MARY COX
1729
oil on canvas
50 $\frac{1}{2}$ X 40 $\frac{1}{2}$"
The Metropolitan Museum of Art, New York. Marquand Fund,
1936

Pieter Breugel the Elder
THE WEDDING DANCE
c. 1566
oil on canvas
47 X 62"
The Detroit Institute of Arts. City of Detroit Purchase

Gustav Klimt
FULFILLMENT, cartoon for the Stoclet Frieze
c. 1905
tempera, gold, and silver on paper
76 $\frac{3}{8}$ X 47 $\frac{5}{8}$"
Osterreichisches Museum für angewandte Kunst, Vienna
With kind permission of Galerie Weiz, Salzburg
Photograph, Narbutt-Lieven, Vienna

Marc Chagall
FLOWERS OVER PARIS
1967
St. Paul de Vence, Artist's Collection
Photograph: Art Resource

Calligraphy by Calligraphy Studios
NEW YORK

Illustration Research: Ann Levy

Copyright © 1985 by Hugh Lauter Levin Associates, Inc.

First Galahad Books edition published in 1999.

Galahad Books
A division of BBS Publishing Corporation
386 Park Avenue South, New York, NY 10016

Galahad Books is a registered trademark of BBS Publishing
Corporation.

Published by arrangement with
Hugh Lauter Levin Associates, Inc.

Library of Congress Catalog Card Number: 98-75465

ISBN: 1-57866-051-3

Printed in China

Prologue

This book tells the story of
our meeting and of our marriage.

As the years go by, the
memories gathered here will help
us recall that wonderful time
when we learned to know each
other, grew to love each other,
and came to be joined together
as husband and wife.

The Bride

Name _____

Birthdate _____

Birthplace _____

The Groom

Name _____

Birthdate _____

Birthplace _____

COUPLE ABOVE ST. PAUL—Marc Chagall

_____

The Bride

_____   _____
Mother   *Father*
Date of Birth _____   Date of Birth _____
Place of Birth _____   Place of Birth _____

Mother's mother (Bride's grandmother)	Mother's father (Bride's grandfather)	Father's mother (Bride's grandmother)	Father's father (Bride's grandfather)
Date of Birth	Date of Birth	Date of Birth	Date of Birth
Place of Birth	Place of Birth	Place of Birth	Place of Birth

_____
The Groom

_____
Mother
Date of Birth _____
Place of Birth _____

_____
Father
Date of Birth _____
Place of Birth _____

Mother's mother (Groom's grandmother)	Mother's father (Groom's grandfather)	Father's mother (Groom's grandmother)	Father's father (Groom's grandfather)
Date of Birth	Date of Birth	Date of Birth	Date of Birth
Place of Birth	Place of Birth	Place of Birth	Place of Birth

When We First Met

I wish I could remember the first day,
First hour, first moment of your meeting me,
If bright or dim the season, it might be
Summer or Winter for ought I can say.

                                    Christina Rossetti

When we met _____

Where we met _____

Who introduced us _____

My first impression of you _____

_____

_____

_____

Your first impression of me _____

_____

_____

_____

THE LOVERS—Pablo Picasso

Our First Date

When _____

_____

Where _____

_____

How we spent the time together _____

_____

_____

_____

_____

The Wooing and the Winning

How do I love thee? Let me count the ways.
I love thee to the depth and breadth and height
My soul can reach, when feeling out of sight
For the ends of Being and ideal Grace.

Elizabeth Barrett Browning

What we did together _____

_____

Places we went together _____

_____

What I came to love about you _____

_____

What you came to love about me _____

_____

The Proposal

Come live with me and be my Love
And we will all the pleasures prove
                              Christopher Marlowe

When it happened _____

Where it happened _____

You said _____

_____

And I said _____

_____

12

THE BETROTHAL—Lucas van Leyden

We Announce Our Engagement

The first people we told _____

_____

Their reaction was _____

_____

Other people we told _____

_____

Their reactions _____

_____

_____

_____

_____

_____

_____

_____

_____

Paste formal announcement or newspaper announcement here,
or describe other ways that news of the engagement spread.

When purchased _____

Where purchased _____

Description _____

_____

_____

_____

Engagement Gifts

Name	Address	Gift

We Pick Our Patterns

Stores Where We Registered _____

_____

China _____
$\qquad$ Pattern $\qquad\qquad$ Manufacturer

Crystal _____
$\qquad$ Pattern $\qquad\qquad$ Manufacturer

Silver _____
$\qquad$ Pattern $\qquad\qquad$ Manufacturer

Other Patterns (Stainless, Barware, Holloware, etc.)

_____

_____

_____

HYDRIA; WOMAN AND EROS (BRIDE RECEIVING PRESENTS)
Attributed to The Washing Painter

The Ceremony

The date _____

The place _____

The time _____

The Ceremony

Special readings _____

_____

_____

_____

Special vows _____

_____

_____

_____

The Bride's Attendants _____

_____

_____

The Groom's Attendants _____

_____

_____

Other Members of the wedding party _____

_____

_____

A MARRIAGE PROCESSION PASSING THROUGH A BAZAAR
Bilaspur or Mandi (India)

The Reception

Where _____

When _____

Color scheme _____

Description _____

_____

_____

_____

Paste Invitation Here

Who Helped Us

The Florist

Name _____

Address _____

Description of flowers ordered:

Places

Ceremony _____

Reception _____

People

Bride _____

Bride's attendants _____

Groom _____

Groom's attendants _____

Other members of the bridal party _____

_____

A COUNTRY WEDDING—Grandma Moses

In charge of food and drink

Name _____

Address _____

_____

Reception Menu

_____

_____

_____

_____

_____

_____

_____

Who Helped Us

The Photographer

Name _____

Address _____

_____

Formal portraits sent to

_____

_____

Candid shots sent to

_____

_____

Other pictures by

_____

_____

Guest List and Gifts

Name   Address   Gift

THE WEDDING—Henri Rousseau

Guest List and Gifts

Name	Address	Gift

Guest List and Gifts

Name	Address	Gift

Description   Where purchased

_____

_____

_____

_____

_____

_____

_____

_____

_____

THE TROUSSEAU—Charles Webster Hawthorne

The Bridal Gown

Gown purchased at or made by _____

Description _____

_____

Accessories

    Veil or Headdress _____

    Shoes _____

    Other _____

Something old _____

Something new _____

Something borrowed _____

Something blue _____

Groom's attire _____

_____

Groom's attendants _____

_____

Bride's attendants _____

_____

Attire of other members of the processional

_____

_____

The Bonds of Marriage

Come let us now resolve at last
To live and love in quiet;
We'll tie the knot so very fast
That time shall ne'er untie it.

John Sheffield

The Marriage License

When procured _____

Where procured _____

The Wedding Rings

Description _____

Purchased at or made by _____

MARRIAGE LICENSE—Norman Rockwell

Bridal Shower

Given by _____

When _____

Where _____

Type _____

Guests and gifts

_____

_____

_____

_____

Pre-Wedding Festivities

Luncheon for Bride's attendants

Where _____

When _____

Gifts to bridal attendants _____

_____

Bachelor Dinner

Where _____

When _____

Gifts to groom's attendants _____

_____

The Wedding Rehearsal

Where _____

When _____

The person in charge _____

The Rehearsal Dinner

Given by _____

Where _____

When _____

Attended by _____

_____

_____

THE JEWISH BRIDE—Rembrandt van Rijn

That Special Day

Weather _____

_____

Headlines _____

_____

President _____

_____

Our favorite song _____

_____

Latest fad _____

_____

44

That Special Day

The Bride's Day

The day's schedule _____

_____

Thoughts and feelings _____

_____

Final preparations and dressing _____

_____

The Groom's Day

The day's schedule _____

_____

Thoughts and feelings _____

_____

Final preparations and dressing _____

_____

Seating and Processional

Music while guests arrived

Played by _____

Instrument _____

Selections _____

Processional

Music for processional _____

Order of processional

_____

_____

_____

THE WEDDING OF STEPHEN BECKINGHAM AND MARY COX
William Hogarth

The Ceremony

My true love hath my heart, and I have his;
By just exchange one for the other gives.

Sir Philip Sidney

Officiated by _____

Assisted by _____

Taking the vows: what we remember most

_____

_____

_____

_____

The Recessional

Selection _____

Played by _____

Instrument _____

Order of recessional _____

_____

The Receiving Line

Where we stood _____

Members of the party _____

_____

Memorable comments _____

_____

Paste photograph here

Now all is done: bring home the bride again;
Bring home the triumph of our victory:
Bring home with you the glory of her gain;
With joyance bring her and with jollity.
Never had man more joyful day than this,
Whom heaven would heap with bliss,
Make feast therefore now all this live-long day.

Edmund Spenser

Number of people attending the reception _____

Our fondest recollections of the reception

_____

_____

_____

_____

_____

The Reception

Music supplied by _____

The music for our first dance _____

Other music played _____

_____

_____

Toasts and Speeches

_____

_____

_____

_____

THE WEDDING DANCE—Pieter Breugel the Elder

The Reception

The Wedding Cake

Paste photograph of the wedding cake here

Wedding cake made by _____

Description _____

_____

54

When I threw the bridal bouquet _____

_____

Who caught it _____

Her reaction _____

_____

When I threw the garter _____

_____

Who caught it _____

His reaction _____

_____

The Honeymoon

When we left _____

Where we went _____

How we traveled _____

How long we stayed _____

Memories of our honeymoon _____

_____

_____

_____

_____

FULFILLMENT—Gustav Klimt

Our First Home

I will make a palace fit for you and me
Of green days in forests and blue days at sea.

Robert Louis Stevenson

Paste photograph of your first home here

Where we lived _____

Description _____

_____

58

True love is but an humble, low-born thing,
And hath its food served up in earthen-ware;
It is a thing to walk with hand in hand
Through every-dayness of this work-day world.

James Russell Lowell

My daily routine _____

_____

His daily routine _____

_____

What we enjoyed _____

_____

Our first quarrel _____

_____

Our first dinner party _____

_____

Our first house guest _____

_____

Our first new piece of furniture _____

_____

FLOWERS OVER PARIS—Marc Chagall

Our First Anniversary

How we celebrated _____

_____

_____

His gift to me _____

My gift to him _____

Other gifts received _____

_____

_____

How we celebrated

First	Paper	
Second	Cotton	
Third	Leather	
Fourth	Fruit / Flowers	
Fifth	Wood	
Sixth	Candy / Iron	
Seventh	Wool / Copper	
Eighth	Bronze / Pottery	
Ninth	Pottery / Willow	
Tenth	Tin / Aluminum	
Fifteenth	Crystal	
Twentieth	China	
Twenty-fifth	Silver	
Thirtieth	Pearl	
Thirty-fifth	Coral	
Fortieth	Ruby	
Forty-fifth	Sapphire	
Fiftieth	Gold	
Fifty-fifth	Emerald	
Sixtieth	Diamond	

When you are old and gray and full of sleep,
And nodding by the fire, take down this book,
And slowly read, and dream of the soft look
Your eyes had once, and of their shadows deep.

William Butler Yeats